Blackpool Trams
Pictorial No. 4

2009 marks the 75th anniversary of the Streamlined fleet, so the fourth book in this series seems an opportune way to celebrate the occasion. The first Railcoach (car 200) actually arrived in Blackpool in June 1933, but the year 1934 saw the first Boat car (car 600 today), open top double decker (car 700 today) and enclosed double decker (car 713 today). The construction of the new fleet was well underway. The period 1933 to 1939 was the most significant in Blackpool tramway history and many fine tramcars built at that time still exist today.

Although primarily concentrating on the cars built in the 1930s, I've also incorporated images of Coronations, Standards and other types which have run in Blackpool. Similar to the previous volumes in this series, this is not a detailed history book. The history of the tramway has been covered in great detail over and over again. I'm not going to tell you that the double deckers are called Balloons and that the trams run to Fleetwood - I hope you already know this! What I have done, once again, is compiled a variety of previously unseen and unpublished images and written specifically about the tram pictured and its surroundings. As well as the familiar promenade shots, I've also included some unusual and rare pictures.

I am indebted to the people who have supplied images and/or information to make this book possible. In particular I would like to thank Brian Turner, Geoff Lumb, Vic Nutton and Tony Wilson (TLP) for the use of their images and to David Umpleby, Paul Turner and many regular contributors to TRAMS magazine who have helped with dates, details and facts. A special thank you goes to my wife, Mary, for her constant support and to Jason Prescott, the man in charge of making all these images come to life.

Enjoy the book.
Nick Meskell
June 2009

Printed by Amadeus Press, Cleckheaton.

Cover: The original Railcoach in the early 1960s in North Albert Street, Fleetwood working a journey to North Station. When it comes to tramcar design, the Railcoach had it all! *(TLP)*
Opposite: A typical winter day on Blackpool seafront in 1965. The Tower, Woolworths and a lonely Brush car heading for Starr Gate. *(Geoff Lumb)*

BRUSH CARS

In 1937, Walter Luff, the General Manager of Blackpool Corporation Tramways completed his moderisation plan. With twelve 'Boat' cars, twelve 'Sun Saloons', thirteen 'Open Top Streamliners', fourteen 'Balloons' and 45 'Railcoaches' all constructed by the English Electric company of Preston, he turned to the Brush company of Loughborough for twenty further Railcoaches, thus completing the purchase of 116 brand new tram cars. Built more or less to the same design as the EE cars, the Brush variety came on stream for the 1937 season, essentially to replace the lost capacity caused by the closure of the Lytham St. Annes tramway. With their swingover seats, sunshine opening roofs and air operated sliding doors, these twenty cars soon became the mainstay of the North Station to Fleetwood route, based at Bispham depot. Although fondly remembered from their days running along Dickson Road, these trams have now spent more years based at Rigby Road depot, working the Starr Gate to Fleetwood promenade route! Seven of the original cars were withdrawn from passenger service by the mid-1980s with two of them, 624 and 628 becoming works cars and 635 being purchased for preservation. With 633 rebuilt as the Illuminated Trawler, the other twelve cars were still in regular passenger service until the end of the 2004 season when all except four (622, 626, 630 and 631) were withdrawn or to use the politically correct term - 'mothballed'. To mark the 70th anniversary of these trams in 2007, car 623 was reinstated and painted in the attractive 'wartime' livery. From the twenty built, just the five cars were considered serviceable members of the fleet at the start of the 2009 season.

Left: Displaying the slanted destination of 'North Station Blackpool', car 291 leaves the promenade at Gynn Square and heads for the short incline to Dickson Road. If you had to describe the North Station route and the tramcars which ran along it in the late 1950s and early 1960s, well, here it is! 291 was one of just five Brush cars that had received the single destination screen modification prior to the closure of this line in 1963 and this image was taken circa 1959. At this time, during the peak summer, thirteen cars were allocated to service, running a five minute headway with alternate cars running from North Station to Cleveleys and Fleetwood. Today there is a huge roundabout here! *(TLP)*

Right: Relegated from their traditional role in 1963, the Brush cars were rehoused at Rigby Road depot and became regulars on the promenade route all year round. Looking not too dissimilar from its days based at Bispham, 289 basks in the late afternoon sunshine at Fleetwood Ferry prior to the 50 minute journey back home. The most obvious difference is, of course, the orange trolley tower which became standard during repaints from 1963 until 1970. Although undated, this image comes from the 1964-1968 period, prior to renumbering. For the record, 291 became 628 whereas 289 is 626 and looking nothing at all like this today, still survives and is considered to be part of the operational fleet. *(TLP)*

The early 1970s were an interesting period for the Brush cars. While the remaining Railcoaches were rebuilt into OMO cars and a lot of attention and time was focused on the conversion of Balloon 725 into Jubilee car 761, some of the Brush cars received works attention. Many had not been through the works since their days on the North Station route. With the demise of the Coronations, the Brush cars were back on all year service from the late 1960s, into the early 1970s and until the introduction of the OMO cars. Any car that sustained serious accident damage or was just simply in a poor condition was withdrawn from service. This led to the demise of 624 in 1971, 629 in 1972 and 635 in 1974. One of the highlights from this period was the 'Tigerrific' advert applied to 622. Although it has featured before in this series, the impact the tram had was quite staggering. In 1975, after nearly four decades of service entirely in the various green and cream liveries, the mould was broken as a multi-coloured tramcar hit the rails. The photo opposite shows the contrast in styles. 621 looks ancient in the corporate green and cream with twin destination screens compared to its audaciously turned out 'modern' sister! The conversion to the single destination screen was usually done during overhaul and in 622s case it was done prior to receiving this advert in June 1975. The conversions started as early as July 1957 when 288 (625) was reworked. It was completed 23 years later when 621 was 'singled' in November 1980. *(Nick Meskell collection)*

A sunny day at Talbot Square in June 1975 with 637 on specials heading south to Pleasure Beach. With the OMO conversion programme almost fully completed, Brush cars had been relegated to seasonal duties for the second time in their lives and although they still worked on Fleetwood service, this was mainly during the early season and Illuminations. This particular journey probably started at Bispham with the tram slotting in between the service cars, giving a 48-seat boost to North prom and then short prom journeys to the fairground. At this time, inspectors were based at Bispham, Talbot Square and Pleasure Beach and these three men were in charge of all the trams on specials. The fashions of the mid-1970s are all too evident looking at the four people to the right of the tram and with Showaddywaddy dominant in the music charts in summer 1975, memories of those wide collars and bell-bottomed trousers come flooding back! Note the Midland Bank, far right. In 1970 ten of the remaining fifteen serviceable Coronation cars received roof-mounted advertising boxes. The boxes ran the full length of each half saloon and included end advertisement panels as well. These boxes were illuminated at night and were short lived despite the extra revenue they created for the tramway. By 1972 just one car (663) retained them with the remainder being transferred to Brush cars and Railcoaches. 637 was one of the recipients and they really changed the whole look of the car. In half green/half cream with cream doors, six sets of numbers and four BCT crests, this was your typical Brush car from that era. *(Geoff Lumb)*

Over the years a number of Brush cars have been used for experimental purposes. As early as 1946, after less than a decade in service, car 303 - the last one built - was used to test a new type of bogie and was fitted with VAMBAC equipment. Lesser projects included the fitting of fluorescent lighting to car 301 and in 1957, car 288 (now 625) became the first with the single destination screens at each end. The latter was one of the more successful trials. Of all twenty cars, 638 was without a doubt the most rebuilt example when in 1969/70, it was converted to one man operation. Although unsuccessful for numerous reasons, the experience gained was crucial in the rebuilding of Railcoaches to OMO cars. When the research was finished, 638 returned to regular service but retained many unusual fittings from the rebuild. Note the small rubber mounted window at the top of a single panel where the former electrically operated single leaf entrance door used to be and three rather than four side roof windows in the front half. On the centre platform (which was the exit), note the grab rail which would have been used by passengers to climb the extra step, unusually sited in the middle of the platform. Taken circa 1977, 638 is spare in depot. The tram last ran during the 1980 Illuminations. *(Nick Meskell collection)*

Above: At the end of the 1971 Illuminations Brush car 624 was withdrawn from passenger service and allocated to the Permanent Way Department. Still retaining many original features such as sliding doors and Crompton-West controllers, the tram took over from Railcoach 221 which in turn became an OMO car. Initially wearing the half green/cream livery of the day, the tram latterly gained this all over green livery and spent the next 35 years performing works duties. Ironically, this was one year longer than it ran as a passenger car! Working alongside 624, as a Railcrane, were the remains of Brush car 628. Withdrawn in 1969, 628s body was scrapped, leaving the underframe for future use and from 1973, the new 628 became part of the Works fleet, allocated the number 751. In April 1985, 624 was renumbered 748, bringing it into line with other cars in the Engineering fleet and then in October 1986, upon bus deregulation, the main tram fleet was transferred to the ownership of Blackpool Transport while Blackpool Council retained ownership of both 748+751 which then became 259+260. It should always be remembered that Blackpool Council owns Blackpool Transport! Into the 21st Century, 259 was used less each year and as the requirement for a dedicated tram passed, it was acquired for preservation by the Lancastrian Transport Trust (LTT) in early 2006. The photo above shows 259+260 on typical duties in Thornton Gate yard in February 1987. *(Brian Turner)*

Inset: As mentioned above, 624 ran with the number 748 in 1985/86. Showing the phony 'Tour of Illuminations' on its twin blinds, 748 pushes 751 through Little Bispham in early 1986. *(Nick Meskell)*

Following the withdrawal of 638 in 1980 the Brush cars went through a period of stability with little change. Thirteen trams were in regular service with 626, 630 and 631 all receiving 'super' overhauls. During the 1980s, all cars received advert liveries of some description and again, until 2004, these trams were the main choice for such advertising schemes. This is summer 1991 with cars 633 and 630 at Pleasure Beach working specials. In the days before window vinyls, both cars look attractive and eyecatching with 630, in a colour scheme not too dissimilar from today, advertising 'Pleasure Beach' while 633 advertises an attraction at the other end of the prom, 'Coral Island'. In 1991, six crew single deckers were required for Fleetwood service each day. There was no timetabled Cleveleys service as such so the remainder were available for use on specials as required. 630 is still in service today as too is 633 although the latter is the Illuminated Trawler! *(Nick Meskell)*

Prior to the 'super' overhauls of the 1990s, 637 became the last Brush car to receive what could be described as a heavy overhaul. This was completed in September 1990 and the tram returned to service for the final weeks of the 1990 Illuminations in a smart green and cream livery, complete with roof advert boxes. Seven months later (in April 1991), the tram was painted into this livery. Remarkably, no sooner had the tram been put to work on the prom, 'Cocos' went bust! This left Blackpool Transport with a newly painted but redundant advert livery. (Did they ever get paid?). There's no doubt that the Illuminated roof advert boxes completely changed the look of the Brush car. Although they may spoil the original curves of the tram, they were a great revenue booster, particularly when used with an all over advert livery. With a pantograph, bus seats and rubber mounted saloon windows, 637 looks very smart and modern and despite all these features and the 1990 overhaul, the tram was withdrawn from service in 2004. 637 is at Bispham in June 1991. *(Nick Meskell)*

For the last two decades or so, 636 has been a popular tram amongst enthusiasts. The car retained many original fittings and with its swingover seats and side roof windows it is, allegedly, in the best condition of all the unrefurbished cars. In addition to this, 636 seems to have been selected for some of the more stylish advert and fleet liveries in the last twenty years. These have included the attractive 'Warburtons Bread' adverts from the 1980s and in June 1989, the tram received a version of the 'wartime' green and cream. More recently (November 2003) the tram received Line 14 Metro livery.

Top Left: An early 1970s view of 636 at Fleetwood Ferry. Sporting another variation of roof boxes, amazingly these were carried by Coronation 664 and the Illuminated Blackpool Belle prior to being refitted to 636! The tram wears the simple green and cream livery from the day including gold fleet numbers (just on the cab ends). *(TLP)*

Bottom left: A very sorry looking 636 in depot on road 14 in 1979 following an accident in which the tram was squashed between OMO 2 and 710! The destination 'ROSSALL' was probably wound on for the photo. Note 634 adjacent in its 'Seagull' livery and a slight glimpse of an orange liveried 603 at the wall end. *(TLP)*

Right: In June 1989, 636 emerged from the Paint Shop sporting a version of the 'Wartime' livery. Although not altogether correct - this was actually the Railcoach version and the wrong shades of green and cream were used - the livery added a bit of variety to what was a very advert dominated tramway. During this period, there was an explosion in advertising vinyls which were affixed to just about everything that moved. Balloons had them on their lower panels (as well as between decks) plus certain Brush cars and Railcoaches were also treated. For 636, the tram advertised 'Fylde Coast Rover' tickets. Considering the effort taken to paint the tram in this special livery, it was a shame it could not have been spared the adverts. The side roof windows, half drop windows, traditional lifeguard and cab windscreens are shown to full effect in this image taken at Manchester Square in autumn 1989. *(Nick Meskell)*

SQUARE
636
Stretch the Fylde Coast from Morecambe to Preston with
Fylde Coast Rover
1/3/7 day tickets
Pick up a leaflet from your local
Transport Enquiry Office
GIFTS
FOR ALL

Regular followers of the tram scene will be familiar with Blackpool Transport's 'change of direction' regarding the tram fleet during 2004. Up until this date things had been pretty stable for a good decade with overhauls and repaints part of an ongoing year-on-year programme. 636, for example, was very much part of the operational fleet during 2003 wearing a green and cream livery and at the end of the season, it passed through the Body Shop and Paint Shop, emerging in this striking Metro livery. Although the Metro Coastlines network is all about buses and essentially nothing to do with the tramway (which is shown on the Metro map but Metro tickets are invalid on trams!), a number of cars (sixteen so far) have been painted in these schemes. This is the Line 14 variety. During this works attention, as is evident in the picture, 636 finally had its curved roof windows panelled over although it is believed they remain in situ under the steel panelling! And so, 636 resumed service in spring 2004 and was a regular performer during the season. Despite the repaint, it was hit-listed for withdrawal and last ran in passenger service on Saturday 30th October, working evening specials. Unlike the other withdrawn cars, 636 was chosen as a test vehicle for a new type of bogie. After a lengthy period of inactivity its trolley tower was removed and, unable to move under its own power, was semi-permanently coupled to fellow withdrawn car 637. After various moves around the depot complex, 636s new bogie was fitted and then on Wednesday 22nd November 2006, it was taken by road to the premises of Stored Energy Technology (SET) in Derby where the new bogie was evaluated. On Thursday 8th January 2009 the tram returned and a series of trials took place between Starr Gate and Pleasure Beach. In April these ceased and having been declared surplus by Blackpool Transport, the tram was sold to SET. Its future is unknown at the time of writing. The image above shows 636 on 22nd November 2006 loading up adjacent to the Fitting Shop. The new bogie was hidden behind the black plastic sheet. *(David Umpleby)*

Following the fleet reduction at the end of the 2004 season only the three refurbished Brush cars survived - 626, 630 and 631. The other nine were designated as 'mothballed'. As some cars including 627 and 632 had valid advertising contracts, Blackpool Transport paid for new vinyls which were duly applied to cars 707 and 709. There was a slight twist to the story when the advertisers on 622 - Glyngary, a Warrington based sash window manufacturer - decided to renew their contract. Instead of applying a new vinyl wrap to a double decker, a decision was taken to reinstate 622 and the tram was in regular use during the 2005 season. At the end of the year when the contract expired, again the seemingly unloved and unwanted 622 was destined to join its sisters in store. Remarkably, the car was chosen for a new advert livery and in August 2006 it emerged in a very simple blue and yellow vinyl for 'Pontin's'. It is understood the advert was supplied free of charge in return for Pontin's allowing the Line 1 promenade bus to terminate at their main entrance. The tram ran in 'Pontin's' livery in 2007 and 2008 and despite the loss of cars in better condition, such as 623, 680 and incredibly, the refurbished 626, the tram was selected for use in 2009. On Good Friday 2009, the first day of the spring service, the last three recognised Brush cars - 622, 630 and 631 - were allocated to Cleveleys service. All remaining members are expected to be withdrawn at the end of the 2011 season. It's quite a remarkable achievement that back in May 1975, 622 was selected for the first all over scheme and in May 2009 - 34 years on - the same tram would become the last unrefurbished Brush car in advertising livery. With its swingover seats and simple filament bayonet lighting system, 622 is largely unchanged from its days on the North Station route. This is Little Bispham, Easter Sunday, 12th April 2009 with 622 working route 11. *(Nick Meskell)*

BLUNDELL STREET AND RIGBY ROAD DEPOTS

Built in 1898 on the site of the original 1885 building and controversially demolished in 1983, the tram depot at Blundell Street was the main operating base for the promenade and Lytham Road routes until the Rigby Road complex was built in 1935. Although it was used mainly to store trams from 1945, the building had many roles over the years including part conversion as an ambulance station and a home for various other tram paraphernalia such as rails and spare bogie frames. Following demolition and conversion to a car park, various sections of rail from the five track layout remained visible. These were finally buried under tarmac in 2007 - it only took 25 years! A year later Blackpool Council decided the site was ideal to build a depot for the forthcoming 'Supertrams'. After various new pointwork was laid on the promenade at Foxhall to allow access to the depot, planning permission was submitted and then refused! For the time being anyway, the site of the former depot will remain a car park and these two images are a fine reminder of what a great building it once was. The Rigby Road depot is, of course, still in use today.

Below: The sole surviving Dreadnought tram of 1902 needs no introduction and on this occasion it was being used for an enthusiasts special which included a run along Blundell Street, passing this huge building. This is the southern entrance of the depot which was altered at various times over the years. Note the ornate design and Corporation Tramways tableau. The red Mark III Ford Cortina and cream Mercedes-Benz 200 series certainly add to this scene from 23rd May 1982. *(TLP)*

Opposite: During the years it was used as a store, Blundell Street depot became the bastion of all tram depots. Rarely did the public see inside and very few images of the stored trams have ever come to light. This incredible slide from about 1979 shows Brush car 629 in its final months, heavily cannibalised and ready for the scrap man. To the left are the sorry remains of 714, also heavily stripped and coated in a thick layer of grime. At this time the previously stored 725 was rejuvenated as 761 and back on the prom. Remarkably, 714 was to follow, becoming 762. 629 was completely broken up by January 1980. *(TLP)*

714
629

Opposite: Within the Rigby Road depot complex of today are the various workshops used to maintain, repair and repaint the tram fleet. This is the entrance to the Paint Shop on Saturday 2nd December 1989 with a bit of history in the making. Having been somewhat neglected throughout the 1970s and into the 1980s a decision was taken to refresh the Boat cars with repaints to match the various liveries carried by the bus fleet. 602 was first in the black and yellow 'Handybus' colours.

Below: On the same day that 602 emerged from the Paint Shop, 604 took its place, moving from the Body Shop. As well as much needed body work and a new lick of paint, all five Boats also received two piece windscreens which replaced the original and badly scratched one-piece plastic screens fitted at the end of the 1950s. 604 was painted in the red and white 'Routemaster' colours.

Page 17: Having carried various advert liveries since 1975, 707 was adorned in a new style for 'Pontin's' in March 1990. In addition to being fitted with a pantograph, the tram received two new destination blinds, both of which contained the destination 'PONTINS'. As trams no longer run past the site of the holiday centre the destination was purely for commercial purposes and within a few months both blinds were torn and replaced with ordinary ones. *(Nick Meskell x 3)*

707
PONTINS

Once the Boat cars were completed, Blackpool Transport turned their attention to the seven Twin cars - fourteen vehicles which had also gone many years without a repaint. 671+681, 673+683 and 675+685 all passed through the works in 1990 which saw them emerge in the half green/half cream livery of the day. In February 1991, 672+682 were split with 682 moving into the Body Shop first. After fairly extensive repanelling the tram was moved back into the depot where a remarkable discovery was made. Although the tram had been renumbered from T2 to 682 in 1968, the actual gold transfers 'T2' had remained at the end which was coupled to 672! Presumably, with all the cables and hoses, it wasn't physically possible to scrape off the T2 and apply the new 682! Amazingly, this went unnoticed for 23 years! Moving into the Paint Shop in March, the T2 disappeared under a coat of cream. It is remarkable in many ways that nobody noticed but if they did, it probably didn't matter as the tram was unmistakably 682 towed by 672! One thing it did confirm though is that neither had been painted in over two decades. In February 2003 the pair were the first to be outshopped in the colourful Metro bus livery, Line 1 version. *(Nick Meskell x 2)*

In April 1991, the freshly painted 682 was hauled from the Paint Shop and deposited on the depot track fan by the Diamond T breakdown truck (seen on page 16 pushing 604). Brush car 633 was called upon and coupling to 682, pushed the tram into the depot to await the completion of 672 and ultimately recoupling and the promenade again. This image shows what is probably yet another rare sight, a Brush car towing a trailer! The pairing of 633+682 just doesn't look right! 672 was repainted in May, and also received a set of OMO trucks and a pantograph. 676+686 were next to be overhauled with 674+684 following on and then in January 1992, 677+687 completed the seven sets. For 676+686 and 677+687 this was to be the last overhaul/repaint as the Metro overhauls in 2003/2004 ceased after 675+685. Looking at 682 again, this was certainly a very smart application of the green and cream colours which suited these trailers well. Delivered new to Blackpool in August 1960, T2/682 was merely a baby, just 31 years old in this picture. 2010 will mark its 50th birthday. *(Nick Meskell)*

Above: The author would like to apologise for using the word 'remarkable' to describe so many images in this book, however this is far from just another winter scene of Rigby Road depot with a few trams peeking out. This is Monday 26th February 1990, a day never to be forgotten when a high tide of 32.2 feet was backed by severe gale force winds and gusting in excess of 100mph. By 10.30 on this day the tram service was suspended south of Talbot Square as the tide rose and huge waves crashed on to the promenade. At 11.43, the tide reached its maximum height but by then it was too late. The prom was under three feet of water and the sea had encroached upon Lytham Road, Hopton Road, the tram depot and all the workshops. The pits inside the tram shed were filled with water and despite the best efforts of the depot staff and hundreds of sandbags, the ferocity was too great and the whole area was flooded out. This first image shows roads 16 to 19 with a row of sandbags having little effect on the incoming torrent. OMO car 5 on road 16 with car 10 behind, and 761 on road 17 are standing in water. Unsurprisingly quite a number of trams suffered water damage. *(Nick Meskell)*

Opposite: A general view across the depot front looking at roads 6 to 11. The longer pits on roads 7 to 9 proved useful as they took longer to fill than the others and it has to be mentioned... 736... HMS Blackpool... surely the closest this tram has ever come to sailing the ocean for real! To the right is 623 in its 'ICI Hillhouse' advert livery and then another tram with a water theme, Boat 606 - minus windscreens. On the promenade, damage to tram shelters, railings etc. was very severe and a number of seafront hotels were flooded out. Rising tides may be something for the future and hopefully the new sea defences will keep the big waves at bay, making images like this just another piece of tramway history. *(Nick Meskell)*

736
CIRCULAR TOUR
PRIMESIGHT ADVERTISING
ICI
CLEVELEYS
623
ICI ICI

BOAT CARS

Walter Luff called them 'Luxury Toast Racks' and for 75 years now, these iconic tramcars have carried millions of passengers along the seafront. Whether it be a short ride from Tower to Pleasure Beach, a Circularl Tour, a Tour of the Illuminations or a ride all the way to Fleetwood, the Boat car is the ultimate Blackpool joy ride. From the twelve built, just two were selected for use in 2009, with three in store and a further three in America.

Below: Bispham Station and the centre track circa 1960 with Boat car 230 and its crew enjoying their meal break. Of all the images from the 1960s in this book this is one which could most easily be replicated today as although stored, car 230/604 is still in Blackpool. Wooden poles at each corner and four festoons of white bulbs gave the car contrasting looks; fresh, clean and contemporary in the afternoon sunshine; shadowy, mysterious and enchanting after dark. *(Geoff Lumb)*

Circular tours provided the backbone of Boat car operation pretty much from their inception in the summer of 1934. Numerous variations took place over the years which included journeys around Marton, from Starr Gate to Squires Gate and even along Dickson Road and down Talbot Road. From 1961 tours commenced from just underneath the Tower at the Central Station tram stop and this very busy image shows just that. It's early evening, about 1961, with two Boats on the centre track awaiting their next tours. With their blinds all set and the seats all turned, the crews appear to be looking towards the inspector who in turn is about to be passed by Balloon 248 (711) en-route to Bispham and a Coronation car behind, no doubt Fleetwood bound. A plethora of signs tell would-be passengers where to wait and what to do and it's just possible to make out an all cream Twin car on that Circular Tour placard. Could that be a queue of people to the right of the inspector who, having enjoyed their evening meal at their back street boarding house, fancy an evening cruise along the prom? And why not! I hope they got a 'late key' from the landlady! The hustle and bustle of the promenade, sunshine, Boat cars, a Circular Tour. This is it! This is Blackpool! *(Vic Nutton)*

Opposite right: When looking through images for inclusion in this series of books it was noted how often 603 appeared, usually wedged in at the back of road 14 in the depot, wearing that orange and white livery, perched on a set of 5' 3" trucks and looking rather sad. The special livery was painted in 1976 and the regauged trucks were for use in Philadelphia in the United States Bi-centennial celebrations of that year. The tram returned in 1978 and was subsequently disused prior to its third and final sailing across the Atlantic ocean, leaving Blackpool for good on 19th February 1985. All those images of the car dumped on road 14 are from that 1978-1985 period and the car was even stored for a while in Blundell Street during which it came very close to being scrapped. Forgetting about the orange years in store, here is 603 heading from Lytham Road on to the prom and specials. The crew look very happy! Pre-1968, running as 228, the tram was just another Boat but there seem to be few images of the car post-1972 when it was repainted in the green and cream livery with six sets of these small gold fleet numbers. *(TLP)*

Opposite left: Most tram enthusiasts will probably remember Boat 607 being loaned to the National Tramway Museum in 1985 and duly becoming the first Boat car to operate at this location. The car returned to Blackpool and settled down to regular use in the late 1980s and beyond. In 1994 the tram was retro-fitted with the four corner posts and bunting and then in February 1996 it was painted into an advert livery for 'Travelcard'. The tram remained in regular use until the great cull of November 2004. All five Boats were initially axed but subsequently four of them were revived. 607 was the exception and has been stored ever since. In happier times, the tram heads towards Foxhall en-route to Pleasure Beach. *(TLP)*

Right: 605 was another Boat car neglected for many years and subsequently disused. During a shortage of trolley arms it was the only serviceable Boat in 1984 but was withdrawn in May 1987 and resurrected in March 1990, passing through the workshops for an overhaul and repaint. It still runs today. On Bank Holiday Monday, 26th August 1991 the tram was used for a private hire for the BBC which included a live broadcast from the tram as it ran along the promenade. Decked out in balloons, 605 is seen at Tower after the event. *(Nick Meskell)*

BBC RADIO TWO
605
THE TOWER EXPERIENCE

One of the most unusual Boat journeys of modern times occurred on 29th July 1991 when one was used for a private hire which took it along the rarely used track on Blundell Street, Princess Street and to the Foxhall pub. Although this track gained significant notoriety when it was used daily between January and April 2005, it had largely been disused since the 1960s. Despite occasional use in 1985, Blackpool Transport had repeatedly said no to enthusiast tours or anything else using it and in particular, access via the facing point off the prom was strictly forbidden. Come summer 1991 and the long established Foxhall pub on the corner of Princess Street and the prom was rebuilt. As part of the reopening ceremony, the pub management wanted a tram outside their building! They actually went one step further and paid for an advert livery on Boat car 606. The tram had carried a random blue and yellow livery from its 'Belhaven Beers' advert and subsequent operation at the Glasgow Garden Festival in 1988. This was latterly adapted by the department store 'Hitchens' and then vinyls were applied advertising 'Fylde Coast Rover'. After a bit of remedial attention, it provided the base colours for 'The Foxhall' and the new advert featured cab end and trolley tower slogans. Fine sunny weather blessed the day of the reopening and with the track and overhead wires checked a few days earlier, the invited guests and brass band boarded the tram at Talbot Square at 10.50. As 606 headed south it was presumed the tram would simply turn off at Foxhall and cross the prom but this was not to be. For fear of derailment (and much embarrassment) the tram went the long way round, running to Manchester Square, then Lytham Road, Hopton Road, Blundell Street, Princess Street and Foxhall Square itself. Once outside the pub there were various speeches before the guests went inside for refreshments. Meanwhile, the brass band provided entertainment and for just under an hour, 606 basked in the warm sunshine. Once the event was over, 606 simply retraced its steps and went back on to the prom and specials. This series of images shows the tram running along Blundell Street, around the curve to Princess Street and then outside the pub itself. As far as it is known these are the only photos of this event. It was a great day and a tiny piece of history was made which perhaps became a little more significant when 606 was exported to America in September 2000, in exchange for Standard 147. *(Nick Meskell x 5)*

Lucas
Autocentre
606
The
FOXHALL

FOXHALL
The
FOXHALL

RESERVED
606
The
FOXHALL
BLACKPOOL
TRANSPORT
MAKE TRACKS TO THE FOXHALL
And have a Sly one!
RE-OPENS
29th JULY
7:30
THE NEWEST OLDEST PUB IN BLACKPOOL
THE FOXHALL

TWIN-SCREEN BALLOON CARS

In 2008 Balloon car 717 returned to service following a major 'heritage' overhaul which included the reinstatement of twin destination screens at each end. A decade earlier 700 was also converted back, meaning that for the first time since 1980 there were two Balloons with the traditional front end. The next six images feature Balloon cars with that classic look, a timely reminder of how it used to be. Similar to the Brush cars, the conversion to the single screen completely altered the look of the tram and after starting with car 257 (720) in September 1955 it took 25 years to get through the 25 cars. 722 was the last in August 1980.

Below: Manchester Square in 1960 with a twin screen Balloon car heading south. This unusual livery is a variation of the 'wartime' green and cream but with a cream band between decks to allow advertising. Cars 237, 238, 242, 243, 244 and 246 looked like this in the 1959-1961 period. *(Geoff Lumb)*

Opposite: A powerful shot of car 254 passing Cavendish Road in the early 1960s. Note the additional English Electric nose plaques just below the top deck windows. Usually these are sited below the driver's cab windows on the top of the pointed nose. 254 latterly became 717. *(TLP)*

FORTUNES for FARTHINGS!
WIN EMPIRE £75000
1/4d
TREBLE CHANCE
CAVENDISH ROAD

Mention the fleet number 706 to anybody today and the words 'Princess Alice' and 'open topper' probably spring to mind. Prior to a horrific collision with 705 in July 1980, the tram was very much just another member of the Balloon fleet. New in September 1934, it was one of thirteen 'open top Streamliners' built to replace the Dreadnoughts on promenade duties. Five years on and the outbreak of war in 1939 seriously reduced their workload. So much so, a decision was made to enclose the top decks and between August 1941 and June 1942, all thirteen cars quickly passed through the works. The conversions were done in reverse order, starting with 249 (712) and finishing with 237 (700). 243 (706) was completed in January 1942. Although the converted cars have a few detail differences to the cars that were enclosed from new, all 27 'Balloon' cars were classified as the same and this was the case right through the 1950s, 60s, 70s and into the 1980s. In 1985, 706 returned to open top status and was named 'Princess Alice'. From pantograph operation to hideous advertising liveries, 706 went through some tough times in the 1990s but thankfully the car has looked more authentic since 2004, with its trolley arm, wooden name boards and 1930s livery. Probably all that is missing is conversion back to the twin screen destinations! All the open toppers which were converted during the war retained their twin destination screens and 706 was converted at the end of 1972. This is Starr Gate in about 1970 with 706 rounding the loop on a short journey to Tower. The loop here was laid around 1938 and altered what was a stub end terminus (further back on the prom) into a quick in and out arrival/departure stop without the need to change ends (and the trolley, seats etc). Plans unveiled for the new 'Supertram' system post-2012 will see this become part of the depot complex and trams will not use it in normal service. Instead, a double track end stub with island platform will be built just around the existing curve off the prom. *(TLP)*

Summer 1977, the Queen's Silver Jubilee and days which seemed to last forever. This image somewhat typifies this period. A time when Blackpool still had a huge tourist industry and if you wanted a sun tan, you didn't go to a tanning salon or spray it from a bottle, you came to Blackpool, hired a deck chair and pitched it on the beach! Life seemed simpler in those days and if you stood on the prom, an endless stream of these double deck tramcars would pass you by. This is 722 at Manchester Square in hot pursuit of a Boat car on a journey to Pleasure Beach. Although the traditional twin screen look of the Balloon cars is held in great affection it must be said how difficult it was to read the destinations and none more so than on cars 709 and 722 which received rubber mounted screens in their final years. 'PLEASURE BEACH' really is hard to read, whether crammed up in pencil thin letters or displayed on top of each other, so you can see why the single screens became popular. Note the position of the fleet numbers and BCT crests compared to the previous images. *(TLP)*

BISPHAM
STATION
BISPHAM
BISPHAM
CASINO
714

Opposite: A delightful nocturnal image of 714 at Bispham Station in 1968. About to enter the centre track, reverse and head for depot, the tram is in practically original condition with a full compliment of half drop windows and various other bodyside fixtures and fittings. The tram station itself oozes character and through the open door is an area for inspectors with a drop safe for tram conductors to pay in their takings. Of the 27 Balloon cars just the two did not receive the single screens, 714 and 725, mainly due to their withdrawal at the end of the 1971 season. Looking somewhat forlorn on page 15, 714 spent nine years in store prior to work commencing on its rebuild into a Jubilee car and today this same tram is still a regular through Bispham, running as 762 and named 'STUART L PILLAR' - the man behind the Jubilee car programme. *(Brian Turner)*

Above: In spring 2009 tram signals were installed at Pleasure Beach and Little Bispham to show which direction the points are set upon entrance to the loops. These add to the various traffic lights and earlier versions of tram signals at Cleveleys and Ash Street, but how about these signals on the prom from July 1975? A British Rail type distant signal with its fish tail, black chevron and a red and white home signal? There's a real railway theme going on here with BR symbols, Stephenson's Rocket and a Class 87 in blue livery. This was probably to mark the 150th anniversary of the opening of the Stockton & Darlington Railway which was celebrated with an exhibition at Shildon in August. With yet another variation in fleet number position and destination blind layout, 709 heads a convoy of trams southbound near to St. Chad's Road on south promenade. *(Geoff Lumb)*

SNOW TRAMS

There is something enormously pleasing about Blackpool's trams in the snow. Ask anybody to describe the attractions in Blackpool and probably the beach, the piers, the Tower, the Pleasure Beach, the Illuminations etc. would spring to mind. How about deserted promenades in thick snow with a lonely tramcar battling the elements? Over the years great efforts have been made to keep the trams running during snowy weather and the results of this hard work are shown here.

Below: Talbot Square, New Year's day 1962 and Railcoach 214 stands at the northern terminus of the Marton route, waiting out time until its next journey. The remains of a heavy snowfall are evident as overcoat clad figures pass the various ornamental buildings. This was the last year of the Marton service and as well as the snow, the tram and everything else, here is a tram service on New Year's day! Like many towns and cities across the country, trams (and buses) operated in Blackpool throughout the holiday period at this time, even including a limited service on Christmas day! *(Brian Turner)*

Opposite: The snowfall of December 1981 featured in the third book in this series and here is another image from that period. Talbot Square again, this time on the prom with OMO 12 and a class mate stabled just about as far south as the snow would allow. Due to the depth and severity of the snow, the service was suspended south of this point. This is Tuesday 15th December. *(Brian Turner)*

TALBOT SQUARE
PAY AS
YOU ENTER
12
MIDLAND BANK

Above: For many years 723 was chosen as a plough car and at the end of the Illuminations it was fitted with home-made snowploughs at each end which simply bolted to the front bumpers. Given Blackpool's location and the influence of the Gulf Stream, the town usually escapes severe snow and while the nearby towns of Kirkham and Preston can be snowbound, Blackpool is often simply wet and grey. So much so, 723 could go for many winters without being used. This certainly wasn't the case here, 14th December 1981 on Central prom. 722 is at Tower. *(Brian Turner)*

Opposite: With plough duties transferred to another car, 723 received a major overhaul in 1992/1993 and upon completion it once again saw winter use. Now fitted with saloon heaters, the tram was employed each weekday on the afternoon school special to Ash Street. Following the demise of the OMO cars in March 1993, the Jubilee cars, one of which was previously allocated to this duty, ended up on the normal Fleetwood service and with the 48-seats of a Railcoach insufficient, enter 723. This is Anchorsholme traffic lights on 16th February 1994. *(Brian Turner)*

ASH STREET
723

The last major snowfall on the Fylde coast occurred during the early hours of Sunday 12th March 2006. With snow forecast, Blackpool Transport's Chief Inspector rostered two drivers at 05.00 for plough duties and with cars 702 and 708 switched on and ready to go, all that was needed was the white stuff. The forecasters were right and from about 02.00 the flakes started to fall. By 05.00 the tramway was under a thick blanket and at 05.20, car 702 was dispatched. Running at reduced speed, the tram ploughed its way to Fleetwood and although only light in places, there were mini-drifts at some of the more exposed locations. This is Ash Street Fleetwood at first light with a stunning image of 702 heading back south, cutting its way through the raw snow. *(Mary Meskell)*

The second driver took out car 708 at 05.40 and headed for Tower and then Starr Gate. From Starr Gate the car continued to Fleetwood and back to depot. This is Little Bispham on the return journey with the snow still falling. Although nothing like as severe as the 1981 fall, no sooner had the plough cars passed over before a thin layer of snow settled on the rails and in terms of winter, mid-March is a lot different to mid-December for many reasons! The use of 708 on this day was quite significant. Not only was it to plough the snow, but the car was one of a handful of Balloons to be 'mothballed' at the end of the 2004 season, destined never to run again. Nevertheless it was fitted with ploughs in winter 2004/2005 and although not required it retained them the following winter, and on this memorable day the tram ran over the full system just the once. (702 did three trips to Fleetwood and towed the failed 641 to depot). The tram retained ploughs for subsequent winters without being used and at the time of writing (May 2009) is still plough fitted! With full winter closures expected in future years and then 'Supertrams', it would seem 708 is now redundant but for the time being at least, the image below shows that final journey on 12th March 2006. *(Mary Meskell)*

This may sound exceptionally strange but the main reason for rostering those drivers and sending out the plough cars was to keep the service running because the Pleasure Beach was open on the Sunday afternoon for half price pre-Easter rides! Of course, this meant extra people in Blackpool and some of these travelled by tram! Although the snow melted reasonably quickly, the Pleasure Beach park itself was deemed 'too snowy' so for the first time in its history, it couldn't open due to snow! (The 'Big One' rollercoaster in a blizzard sounds fantastic). Despite this setback the service started as normal and although passenger loadings were light, trams ran for a short while until a series of 'weather related' issues caused the failure of a number of Centenary cars. Eventually the tram service was abandoned with buses taking over for the rest of the day. This is 644 heading south past the Manchester pub in blizzard conditions. You can just about make out the Tower in the background. Standing on the prom in such severe weather with his assistant, the cameraman wasn't the only fool to brave the weather. During this photo session a snow-clad jogger passed, wearing just a vest and shorts and he was followed by a guy kitted out in full ski gear including goggles and a pair of skis! *(Nick Meskell)*

Away from the promenade and north of Cleveleys the snow was much deeper, especially across the open fields between Broadwater and Rossall Square. It's the same day, Sunday 12th March and 645 departs from Broadwater during the late morning, prior to its failure. For the record, cars 641, 642, 643, 644, 645, 646 and 647 were allocated to service on this memorable day. 647 was the first tram to Fleetwood, 06.04 from the depot. 762 came into traffic for a short while following the early demise of 641. 702 and 708 can also be added to the used list. By Monday morning the snow had melted and everything was back to normal. Of course, it will snow in Blackpool again, but this was almost certainly the last 'snow day' with the existing fleet and the Balloon plough cars. *(Nick Meskell)*

ILLUMINATED CARS

Below: It's probably against the law to compile a pictorial book on Blackpool's trams and not include some of the Illuminated fleet so here goes. 'TRAMNIK ONE', the Rocket, stands adjacent to the Fitting Shop wall on Blundell Street prior to duty on 27th October 1963 - ironically the last day of the North Station route. Built just two years earlier, this iconic tramcar was in regular use each autumn until 1999. It was donated to the Lancastrian Transport Trust in 2002. *(Geoff Lumb)*

Opposite: Friday 18th October 1963 and the Hovertram runs along Hopton Road heading for the prom and another evening of tour duty. It is often said that the best time to see Blackpool's Illuminations is after rainfall as the reflections on the wet roads and pavements are superb. Here is the proof! This was the second season for the 'Go Well - Go Shell' tram and of all the Illuminated cars ever built, the seating capacity of 99 was the highest ever attained. *(Geoff Lumb)*

SHELL
GO WELL - GO SHELL

SENIOR SERVICE
TIPPED
The best filter tipped cigarette
4'2
ABC
CO

Opposite: Taken just a few minutes prior to the Hovertram on page 41, the original Western Train also heads for the promenade and tour duty on this wet October evening. These delightful tramcars were without a doubt the pride of the fleet, bringing smiles to the faces of millions of children and adults during their 37 years of service. Withdrawn in 1999 and unceremoniously dumped at the back of the tram shed, that really was the end.....or was it? *(Geoff Lumb)*

Below: Never say never and after almost ten years out of traffic and a two year major overhaul, 733+734 were back on the promenade in May 2009. This is the evening of Tuesday 12th and the first official outing for these trams. Restored to near original condition complete with the 'ABC TELEVISION' sponsorship this £320,000 overhaul, partly financed by the Heritage Lottery Fund, has returned this iconic machine to its rightful place. Welcome back! *(Nick Meskell)*

CORONATION CARS

For numerous reasons they were not the most successful tramcars to ever operate in Blackpool but there's no doubt that the Coronation class of 1952 brought a new standard of excellence to the Blackpool scene. The words handsome, spacious and fast are often used to describe them and similar to the Centenary cars of today they are often remembered for all the wrong reasons.

Top left: Although not shown, this is believed to be Coronation car 304 under construction at the Roberts factory in Wakefield. Resting on wooden blocks, the extraordinarily huge steel body is shown to full effect.

Top right: Same tram, same location a few weeks later almost fully panelled and glazed. The slanted 'North Station Blackpool' destination was never shown for real.

Opposite: Pickfords built a special low loader for the conveyance of the Coronations. This is September 1952 with 307, the fourth car, arriving in the Bus Yard at Rigby Road. *(Geoff Lumb collection)*

In 1949 when Walter Luff was proposing a new class of tramcar he told Blackpool Council that he needed 120 crew members to operate twenty double deckers on a two shift basis whereas with 120 crew he could man thirty single deckers instead. Other factors such as greater speeds and lower costs were also cited. Based on a seated capacity of 84 plus six standees those twenty doubles could offer a total capacity of 1800 at any time whereas the thirty singles, seating 56 passengers with a further twenty standees on the large platforms and wide aisles was 2280 - clearly a lot better value for money. Of course, in the end just 25 cars were ordered and despite their greater size, the number of standing passengers was capped at six. This latterly prompted the top deck end bench seats on the double deckers (fitted from 1957) which increased their capacity by ten. 22nd May 1960 at Little Bispham with car 322 about to depart the loop for South Promenade. *(Geoff Lumb)*

Below: Despite all their problems, the Coronation cars brought a whole new level of comfort and speed to the tramway in the early and mid-1950s. With their faster acceleration and greater speeds, the bigger cars with their wider aisles were appreciated by passengers. Based at Rigby Road, they operated all year round on the Starr Gate to Fleetwood service which until 1963, was supplemented by the North Station to Fleetwood service. Although perfectly good trams, the twenty year old Brush cars were clearly a generation behind and passengers soon learned this fact. In the image below cars 317 and 328 pass outside the Cliffs Hotel on a fine sunny evening circa 1960. By this time, the cab end aluminium mouldings on both cars had been modified to just a simple strip. Fleetwood has, of course, always been Fleetwood but Starr Gate was still being referred to as South Promenade at this time. *(TLP)*

Opposite: By 1968 and the fleet renumbering the Coronations were a very different breed. The first car (313) had already been withdrawn and at the end of the Illuminations, four more cars were stopped. This is June 1968 with contrasting styles at Lowther Avenue tram stop. Still working on Fleetwood service (and South Promenade now known as Starr Gate), the (nearly) all cream and VAMBAC fitted 648 passes the half green/half cream 663 with its Z4 controllers. 648 was one of the cars axed at the end of the season while 663 survived until 1974 and is preserved today. Some fifteen years after their introduction and despite everything, Coronations could still be found on all year service. During the mid 1960s the winter service was every twenty minutes from Starr Gate to Fleetwood and every twenty minutes Tower to Fleetwood thus giving a ten minute headway and it was worked mainly by Brush cars and Railcoaches with occasional appearances by Coronation cars with Z4 controllers. *(Brian Turner)*

FLEETWOOD
648
STARR GATE
663

THE MARTON ROUTE

Above: The Marton route is still held in great esteem by many tram enthusiasts and looking at these five images, it's quite obvious why. A busy scene in Abingdon Street with a VAMBAC car on the corner of Clifton Street just a few minutes into the journey from Talbot Square. From the departure stop at Talbot Square, the trams had to contend with two gentle gradients, firstly along Clifton Street itself and then along Church Street for a short while. Note 'H. Hunter Ltd' behind the tram and the horse and jockey tableau. As well as a 'Ladies Department', the company were 'Hosiers' and 'Hatters'. *(Vic Nutton)*

Below: Church Street circa 1960 with an unidentified Railcoach on the climb past St. John's Church and the Hippodrome. Local residents and visitors may well have travelled by tram to see Johnny Mathis, the Texas born singer, songwriter and actor who along with fellow patriot Rose Marie, were appearing live at this venue. Note the position of the driver's windscreens, it must have been a warm day! *(Vic Nutton)*

Opposite: This truly delightful image taken just a bit further along Church Street shows a VAMBAC car heading towards Talbot Square, passing the majestic gardens of The Citadel. Although there is no information with this slide, the lack of external beading on the tram would suggest it was either car 15 or 21 as both looked like this in their final years. Note the bamboo trolley pole fixed to the overhead pole nearest to the camera and the white steel route card in the driver's side window. Journey time from South Pier to Talbot Square was 23 minutes. The same journey along the direct promenade route took about 12 minutes.
(Vic Nutton)

Even today, if you stand outside the tram depot at Rigby Road, sooner or later a tram will appear and this was the case at Marton depot in June 1961. Look closely though, how many images have you ever seen of a gathering of cars outside this particular depot without any VAMBAC cars? Railcoach 266 heads for Talbot Square, 283 heads for South Pier while 212 is having its trolley turned, having just come from the depot, with another Railcoach standing behind. Note the tram shelter, polo-type tram stop sign and three well dressed gentleman sitting on a bench. *(Brian Turner)*

Opposite left: Taken just a few minutes earlier than the image opposite and bit further south towards Watson Road with a Railcoach and Brush car passing each other, the latter being chased by a Lytham St. Annes bus. Again, the cleanliness of the scene relates to simpler times. Considering the length of this line, there were a total of six crossovers: Manchester Square (on Lytham Road itself prior to the junction for the depot), St. Chad's Road, Royal Oak, Station Road, Watson Road and Highfield Road. A seventh crossover was situated at the end of Lytham Road, although technically, it was part of the terminus, used by all cars to reverse. Serving the large area that it did, the service along here was excellent. In the mid-1950s, for example, on a weekday the first car was 06.11 from Squires Gate and then every five minutes, alternating Cabin (Railcoaches and Balloons) and Bispham (Railcoaches and Brush cars). Last through car was 23.00 to Bispham and the very last departure was 00.03 as far as Manchester Square. *(Vic Nutton)*

Opposite right: The short section of track between Royal Oak (Waterloo Road) and Station Road was shared between the Lytham Road cars and Marton cars during the season. It was also the only place on the entire Blackpool tram network where every example of the Streamlined fleet could be seen. With Railcoaches, Brush cars and Balloons on the Lytham Road service, VAMBACs and Railcoaches running around Marton and Boat cars on their Circular tours, this very short piece of track with its double junction at either end really was a tram 'hotspot'. The image opposite, also taken on 13th August 1961, (in the rain!) highlights the three types of car seen most often. To the left, VAMBAC 15, is about to take the right curve into Waterloo Road. To the right, Balloon 262 (probably running late) on a journey from Cabin to Squires Gate is caught up by an unidentified Railcoach on a Bispham to Squires Gate service. How late the Balloon actually was would determine if the car continued to Squires Gate or turned short. The usual turning point would be Highfield Road. Although the promenade and Lytham Road routes ran virtually parallel from Manchester Square to the Blackpool boundary at Squires Gate/Starr Gate, the timetables were very different. For example, with Lytham Road clearly serving local residents and the prom serving holidaymakers, the first tram from Starr Gate (in summer 1956) wasn't until 08.24 Mondays to Saturdays and as late as 09.24 on Sundays. On Lytham Road, as mentioned above, the first car was 06.11, then 06.25, 06.36, 06.45 and about every ten minutes until the five minute headway commenced from 08.00. On Sundays, the first car was 07.41. Likewise, the frequency - promenade from Starr Gate - every twelve minutes; Lytham Road every five. Naturally, specials would have run to Starr Gate as required. One final point to mention is Balloon 262 which can still be found on the promenade today, rebuilt as 761. *(Vic Nutton)*

RAILCOACHES

In 1933 the 'Railcoach' was the ultimate tramcar. Designed by English Electric for Blackpool, the idea was to match the same comfort and style offered by the luxury motorbuses of that era. Sliding roofs for use on hot days, electric heaters for the winter, chunky upholstered swingover seats on which every passenger faced forward and clocks - they really did think of it all. Even the driver had a separate cab area with twin windscreens, twin headlights and a seat! Luxury indeed! Car 200 was delivered in June 1933 with a further 24 cars in 1934 and 20 more in 1935. With a fleet total of 45, this was the highest single class of tramcar in Blackpool, a number unlikely to ever be surpassed.

Below: From their introduction, Railcoaches were put to work on the Lytham Road route and although supplemented by Brush cars and Balloons, this route really was their own. This is October 1961, the final days prior to closure and car 200 approaches Bloomfield Road. At this time the car was just 28 years old and the closure of this line was not only significant for the loss of route mileage, it was also the beginning of the end for the Streamlined fleet. Up until this time all the trams purchased in the 1930s remained active. In the photo, it's good to see the local barber offering to shave customers! As well as various hair cuts and styles, the word SHAVE is the most dominant. Perhaps that's what's missing in today's society, the opportunity to have a shave on the high street! *(Brian Turner)*

It was often wondered what pre-war holidaymakers to Blackpool must have thought when they stepped off the steam train at North, Central or South stations and stumbled across one of these beasts. Back home, their own trams would probably have wooden seats, open vestibules and no heaters. For tram drivers on holiday in Blackpool, not only did these cars have air brakes, they had a windscreen and, wait for it - WIPERS! This is Little Bispham on 22nd May 1960 with car 213 waiting out time prior to a full length promenade journey. 213 was delivered in January 1934 and although just over 26 years old at this time, the tram still looked magnificent despite showing the strains of all year round service in a seaside town. Thanks largely to the Coronation cars and their problems, 213 dodged the initial cull of cars in 1962 and was kept in reserve until March 1965. It was scrapped inside Bispham depot in October the same year. *(Geoff Lumb)*

LIMITED STOP
RESERVED
275
JE 57

Opposite: In the early 1960s, with the closure of the inland routes imminent, a number of enthusiasts tours took place and many of these used the Vintage cars which were visiting Blackpool for the 75th anniversary in 1960. Cars such as Conduit 4, Rack 2, Dreadnought 59 and the home-based Standards were chosen but one particular tour from June 1961 broke the rules and employed what was at the time one of the latest rebuilds, car 275. In 1957 this ordinary Railcoach was withdrawn from service and rebuilt with flat front ends to be used as a trailer in the Twin car experiment. Towed by sister car 276, also with flat ends, this was the prototype Twin set in 1958. 275s days as a trailer were short lived and with its motors refitted in January 1961, it became a towing car and in time, got its own trailer, T5/685. They say timing is everything in life and in tramway terms, well here it is! 275 on Lytham Road having just turned the corner from Station Road and... *(Geoff Lumb)*

Above: This is one of those photos that can easily baffle people. Starr Gate with Coronation car 308 on the loading stop, perfectly normal for the 1960s but...? This is the same tour, earlier on the same day, and 275 provides what must be one the ultimate gems in Blackpool tram photography. It's the mother of all rare track in Blackpool, the stretch which once linked the Starr Gate terminus to the Lytham Road terminus via Squires Gate Lane. This section of track is actually in the road at Starr gate and fed the junction leading to the former line to St. Annes and Lytham. Amazingly the tram rails and overhead wires were still in situ even though they were last used by the Lytham cars in 1937 – 23 years earlier. Another bizarre fact about this track is that when it fell into disuse the rails were tarred over, and then in 1957 the tar was dug up, exposing them again. They were used for a brief period before being covered over again and are probably still there today! *(Geoff Lumb)*

After the 276+275 experiment of 1958, eight more Railcoaches were selected for the Twin car programme. This was the first serious alteration to the 45-strong fleet since new. With all eight chosen cars taken out of normal service by summer 1961 and then mass withdrawals from October the same year, these were not altogether good times for what were previously the pride of the fleet. This delightful shot at Bispham Station from 19th August 1962 shows 273 and presumably T3 in what was their second summer of operation. Although rebuilt to tow the trailer, 273 still ran as a solo car in the winter and early season. Given the date of 1962, who knows, perhaps it went around Marton alongside the VAMBACs or did a day's work on the North Station route! Note the 'LIMITED STOP' glass above the destination and the position of the crossover which was used by cars running off the northbound (west) track to/from the depot on Red Bank Road. *(Vic Nutton)*

Over the years various efforts have been made to smarten up the the tramway. The alterations carried out in the late 1980s around the lighthouse in Pharos Street, Fleetwood gave the trams their own dedicated section which was block paved and seasonally decorated with flower baskets. And very nice it was too! In addition a new tram stop was sited, as seen to the right of the trailer. This is 674+684 in summer 1990, heading south with a market day special. By this time the once graceful Twin cars (and that Railcoach underneath) had become somewhat forlorn. As mentioned on page 18, these trams went years without a repaint and this is all too evident in this image. Note the plastic self adhesive Blackpool Transport logos, which were applied in 1986 after the BCT crests were crudely painted over. The destination blind, well, it's obviously torn and while stabled at the Ferry the driver only had one thing to do, wind it on to Pleasure Beach, but he forgot and nobody noticed! One design retained by the Railcoaches converted to Twins was the ability to fully open the windscreen. Instead of the wide open two piece design (as on page 52), this single pane of glass could still almost get to 90 degrees! *(Nick Meskell)*

With the ten cars selected and rebuilt as Twin cars by 1961 and the scrap man claiming the majority of the Series 1 cars by 1965, the Railcoach fleet was seriously decimated by this time. Car 209 became the locomotive for the Western Train, 222 was reused, proving the basis for the Hovertram. By 1970, certain cars were stored, one was a Works cars, two had been experimentally rebuilt and just eight examples (all Series 2 cars) were still active - running as genuine Railcoaches. What followed next for these cars was a turning point in history, not only for the trams themselves but the long term survival of the tramway. Enter the OMO cars.

Above: With various plans and funding in place, attention was turned to this wreck - car 616. On 27th June 1970 when 616 was on a journey to Cleveleys, it ran into the back of 673+683 at Cabin. The damage is all too evident in this image, taken soon after arrival back in depot. 616 was destined for the scrap man or perhaps a rebuild of some kind. The latter was the preferred option and along with 610 (withdrawn 1969) and 620 (1970) - both needing works attention, the long stored car 220 (608) and former Works car 221 (609), Blackpool Corporation had a mottley selection of Railcoaches from which to build a new class. These became OMO cars 1 to 5. *(TLP)*

Below: With the conversions in full swing, attention was focused on what were the last six genuine Railcoaches in normal service plus the two rebuilds, 611 and 618. 619 was one of these trams and, withdrawn in April 1972, it was stripped and rebuilt as car 7. This image shows the tram in summer 1972, stored at the back of road 1 in the tram depot awaiting a move into the Body Shop. Another partially rebuilt Railcoach, (probably 617/OMO 6) is stored just in front. *(TLP)*

The five year period between 1971 and 1976 subsequently saw the thirteen surviving Railcoaches rebuilt as OMO cars. Officially they were classified as 'new' as opposed to 'rebuilt' and they were supposed to be known as the 'Seaspray Class'. This never caught on and although occasionally referred to as OMO Railcoaches, they were simply known as OMO cars or just OMOs. Car 9 was rebuilt from 613 and came on stream in time for Easter 1973. It's ultimate claim to fame will always be the fact it was the last car painted in the sunshine yellow and crimson colours. It ran in this guise until August 1976 when a coat of red and cream followed. This is Cocker Square, June 1975 with the tram about to join the road for the passage around the Metropole hotel. The tram is still very much in original, as converted, condition complete with a few bumps and scratches. *(Geoff Lumb)*

STARR GATE

Opposite: With its windscreen wiper clearly doing something wrong, car 1 passes over the exit from the Little Bispham loop on a morning journey from Fleetwood to Starr Gate. Although undated, the livery and external fittings would point to about 1979 or 1980. The OMO cars became synonymous with the Starr Gate - Little Bispham circuit during the summer from 1977 until 1986. Delays to the road traffic in Lord Street caused by the slow pay-as-you-enter procedure prompted a ban on these cars during the peak of the day although they still ran to Fleetwood during the early morning, the evening and of, course, at any time during the winter. *(TLP)*

Below: From Coronation cars, to Brush cars and Railcoaches and then OMO cars - Blackpool Corporation certainly got their money's worth from the roof advert boxes! This delightful image at Talbot Square, also from June 1975, shows a freshly repainted car 4 Fleetwood bound. Built from Railcoach 220, this was a strange tram as unlike many of its sisters, it missed almost a decade of service. Withdrawn and stored in October 1963 the tram was basically forgotten about prior to selection and a rebuild as an OMO car, returning to traffic in October 1972. During this nine year gap most of the other Railcoaches were working all year service. *(Geoff Lumb)*

Above: Car 11 was the last to be rebuilt from what was an original Railcoach, entering service in May 1975. Dated June 1975, the car is less than a month old here and it certainly looks clean and new. The red and cream livery varied slightly for cars 10 and 11 as their trolley towers were painted cream. This was a very typical scene in the mid 1970s. Note the huge facade of Lewis's department store and the 'Adshel' waiting shelter. *(Geoff Lumb)*

Below: It's obvious that the photographer was enjoying a walk along the prom, snapping the OMO cars as he went, as this is the fourth image from the same day, a little further south along the prom, near to Tower. Car 6 stirs up the sand as it glides across Central Promenade, heading for Fleetwood. The summer timetable in operation in the mid/late 1970s employed fourteen cars on what was a ten minute service between Starr Gate and Fleetwood. Nine of these would have been OMO cars with the other five either Brush cars or 678-680. It was traditional to start this service on the Monday before the late May Bank holiday weekend and it continued through until the end of the Illuminations. At some point during late June or early July, the OMO cars switched to the Starr Gate - Little Bispham service by day thus allowing fourteen Balloons to take over the main Fleetwood schedule. It may well have been that by the mid-1970s, a decade after the inland routes had closed, the tram system was a shadow of its former self and by comparison it probably was. Nevertheless during the season there was sufficient demand for a double decker to run to Fleetwood every ten minutes all day every day. With the OMOs in between, a guaranteed and credible five minute headway operated along the prom. *(Geoff Lumb)*

Pictures of the scrapping of any vehicle, whether it be tram, train, bus or coach always seem so vile and grotesque and they don't come much more severe than this. Look again at the pictures of OMOs 6 and 9 previously, that was June 1975; thirteen years later - July 1988 - and it was all over. This is the Bus Yard at Rigby Road with cars 6 and 9 in their final days. Unfortunately the majority of the Railcoaches met a gruesome death just like this and whether 1962 or 1988, the final outcome was always inevitable. Note the gold fleet numbers, peeled Blackpool Transport logo and washed out BCT crest underneath. RIP. *(Nick Meskell)*

Above: Although the introduction of the Centenary cars wiped out most of the OMOs in the late 1980s, a handful survived, largely due to the almost Coronation-like defects of the new class. Of these, four members were painted in a green and cream livery: 1, 5, 8 and 11. It's quite remarkable what these trams actually achieved as in addition to their original role on all year service from 1935 until 1963, they took over from the failed Coronation cars on all year service in the 1964-1972 period. Then, once rebuilt, they were back on all year service in their own right as OMO cars. When their replacements, the Centenary cars, proved a liability they were back on the timetable again until their final demise in 1992/1993. Is that four lives? The loops at Pleasure Beach with cars 8 and 11 on specials in May 1991. *(Nick Meskell)*

Opposite: Seemingly unwilling to die and very much needed at the time, the OMO cars just carried on and on which, by the spring of 1991, prompted what was the last major workshop attention for this class. Car 5 was the subject and emerged in this very stylish one-off green and cream livery. This was its very first day out following the repaint, Saturday 8th June, at Pleasure Beach. *(Nick Meskell)*

PLEASURE BEACH
PAY AS
YOU ENTER
5
TRAMWAY
712
LUCKY NUMBERS

ANYTHING GOES!

The final eight pages of the book feature numerous images which didn't fit into a section within the various chapters, or perhaps they needed a chapter of their own.

Opposite: Bispham Station, July 1968 and it would be possible to have a competition to guess what's going on here! The Coronation car appears to have failed and run down the centre track. The Railcoach, following on the next service has stopped alongside it so the passengers can swap cars. The conductor looks smart in his uniform and it's wondered what the inspector is saying/thinking? The failure rate of the Coronations has been well documented but this proves that even as late as 1968, the cars which retained the VAMBAC equipment were still allocated to the timetabled service. There's something exceptionally ironic about this image, as although this was 1968, you could easily replicate it today. 40 years on, instead of these two, you would have Centenary car 641 and Brush car 630 side by side with the passengers swapping over. The liveries would be different and the staff would be wearing high visibility jackets but the breakdown scenario is exactly the same. One final point to mention, 620 and 308? New and old fleet numbers side by side! *(Brian Turner)*

Page 73: It is often said that following the closure of the North Station route in 1963, the tramway scene in winter was fairly bleak until the early 1970s and the OMO cars. This may well have been the case but not on 27th February 1965 when Standard car 160 was used for an enthusiasts tour. In a scene oozing 1960s nostalgia, the tram rumbles past Manchester Square heading south. *(Geoff Lumb)*

TRAM STOP
ALL CARS
STOP HERE FOR
NORTH SHORE
BISPHAM
CLEVELEYS
FLEETWOOD
QUALITY
WALLER
ANNUAL
CHAMPIONSHIPS

Opposite and below: Enthusiast Vic Nutton was in Blackpool on 13th August 1961 photographing and riding on the trams and Standard 40 was on specials. The car was running up and down the promenade on what was just another busy Sunday in mid summer. While waiting at Central Station (Tower) car 40 suddenly appeared with 'HIGHFIELD ROAD' on its destination blinds and Vic couldn't resist a ride. Once on board it was discovered that the tram had been sent to cover for a missing service car and the reason for turning back at Highfield Road was to get a tram in the correct northbound slot of the absentee. At the destination, all passengers alighted and as shown, the trolley arm was turned and the tram ran over the crossover. While taking the second image, Vic actually missed a ride back on the tram and had to catch the next Railcoach instead! This was exactly 78 days before the line closed. The Standard cars were always associated with the Marton route and as well as the promenade, they ran along Lytham Road at various times in their history. However, with a Railcoach and Balloon stronghold by the late 1950s/early 1960s and the few remaining Standards relegated to seasonal specials, this must rate as one of the most outrageous workings of the final months of the line. Enthusiast specials with various exotic cars traversed this route prior to closure but this was for real, a normal working, as required, on the day, normal passengers and thankfully, recorded here forever.

This is another image, similar to that on page 21, where the reader may be puzzled as to where the tram actually is and what it's doing there. It is, of course, Pleasure Beach, circa 1961 and the cameraman is on the top deck of an enthusiasts tour running around the loop. In front of him is Coronation 321 dumped on what was a partially disused siding. Although still connected to the mainline and wired, there was clearly no exit! The destination blind is set for South Promenade via Pleasure Beach so it looks as if the tram has terminated short and has travelled (or been pushed) around the inner loop and into this siding. Research for this book uncovered other photos of abandoned Coronations in this siding so it would appear to be a regular dumping ground. The tram would either have been repaired and driven empty back to depot or been towed by another car. The delivery of the 25 cars was not even complete before the local media had latched on to their problems. In 1953 an article in *The Gazette* talked about 'screeching brakes' and high profile breakdowns with 'smoke pouring from the ceiling or driver's cabs'. Add to this cracked axles, water ingress and general problems such as excessive weight and high electricity consumption. This was certainly something that Walter Luff got horribly wrong. *(Vic Nutton)*

Two scenes at Pleasure Beach from 1990 showing the spur to the outer loop in use by northbound cars. This is 11th April with 623 (inset) having suffered a smashed pantograph adjacent to the northbound stop. Ironically, this was its first day in service wearing this advert livery! To maintain the service, all trams from Starr Gate travelled over the rarely used spur and onto the outer loop. The incident happened at about 13.15 and it took nearly three hours to make repairs and tow 623 away. The unmistakable OMO 10 is pictured having just entered the curve. Note the Ocean Boulevard complex under construction in the background. *(Nick Meskell)*

A virtually identical incident occurred on 16th September when 644s pantograph (inset) smashed just before the northbound stop. Again, the spur was put to use and this is 647 on its way round. Just to make matters worse, literally seconds after this picture was taken, 677+687 entered the outer loop and 677 derailed, colliding with the concrete fence and an overhead pole. The job was well and truly stopped then! Blackpool Council decided that this spur was no longer needed when the track was relaid in this area during winter 2007/2008 and as a result it was lifted and not replaced. It was used for the last time on Sunday 4th November 2007 when the last few service cars were given special permission to travel over it. Car 700 was the last normal car, followed by 147 as a special. *(Nick Meskell)*

It is probably compulsory to finish a Blackpool tram book with some pictures of Works vehicles so here is another gem from June 1975. It's roads 18 and 19 in the Rigby Road depot with two almost identical overhead line buses and a tram. The buses were bought second hand from Manchester Corporation and were formerly used for maintenance of their trolleybus system. Both were Guy Vixens and 240 (TVM 891) was purchased in November 1965 with 241 (TVM 892) acquired in January 1968. Hidden behind them is car 754, alias Marton 31, which today can be found fully restored and in regular service at Beamish Museum. Of particular interest is the orange single arm Brecknell Willis pantograph mounted centrally on the open work deck. Pantograph trials were taking place at this time which led to 678 being fitted with this single arm type and then in February 1976, OMO 5. *(Geoff Lumb)*

Demolished in 1983 and with the site now occupied by a large supermarket, the tram depot at Bispham was one of three built by the tramroad company in 1897/1898. Used as a running shed for the North Station to Fleetwood route for the majority of its existence, the building consisted of six roads. As an example, in 1960 all 20 Brush cars and the eight surviving Pantograph cars were based there. Pictured on the track fan outside the depot on 22nd May 1960 is Standard car 160 seemingly on its way in from Cabin (?) and in the foreground is Engineering car No.3. The latter was formerly a Standard car, numbered 143 and after withdrawal from service in October 1957, it was modified and took up its new role from July 1958. Initially numbered as just 3, the tram became 753 in 1968 and was in regular service until a fire partially destroyed it in 1990. Acquired by the Lancastrian Transport Trust, at the time of writing the tram is undergoing a major restoration and will return to working order for the 125th anniversary celebrations in 2010. This early image of the car shows it with the top deck front ends still in situ. These were removed in October 1961, making it very similar in appearance to sister car 754. *(Vic Nutton)*

TRAMS magazine, the Blackpool Tram DVD and other tram and railway DVDs

Back cover: If you had to describe a typical summer day in Blackpool in 1970, well here it is! A trio of young ladies carry their suitcases, a man in his best suit, a Balloon car and the Tower. Nostalgic scenes like this remind us all of a long forgotten era but through everything, the trams still remain. *(TLP)*

Published by Train Crazy c/o Videoscene, PO Box 243, Lytham St. Annes. FY8 9DE